The Chort Book of

MW00904744

CHRISTMAS CAROLS

40 Traditional Christmas Carols

arranged especially for Cello.

All in easy keys.

Play-Along Backing Tracks

available online!

Amanda Oosthuizen

Jemima Oosthuizen

The Chortling Cello Series
Wild Music Publications

www.wildmusicpublications.com

We hope you enjoy *The Chortling Cello Book of Christmas Carols!*

Take a look at other exciting books in the series
Including: *Christmas Duets, Trick or Treat – A Halloween Suite, More Christmas Duets,* and more coming soon!

For more information on other amazing books please go to:
http://WildMusicPublications.com

For a **free backing track** to play along to
(using the music from this book) visit:

http://WildMusicPublications.com/secret-67cello-tracks32/

And use the password: HelloCello123

Happy Music-Making!

The Wild Music Publications Team

To keep up –to-date with our new releases, why not
follow us on Twitter

@WMPublications

Contents

Page

Jingle Bells

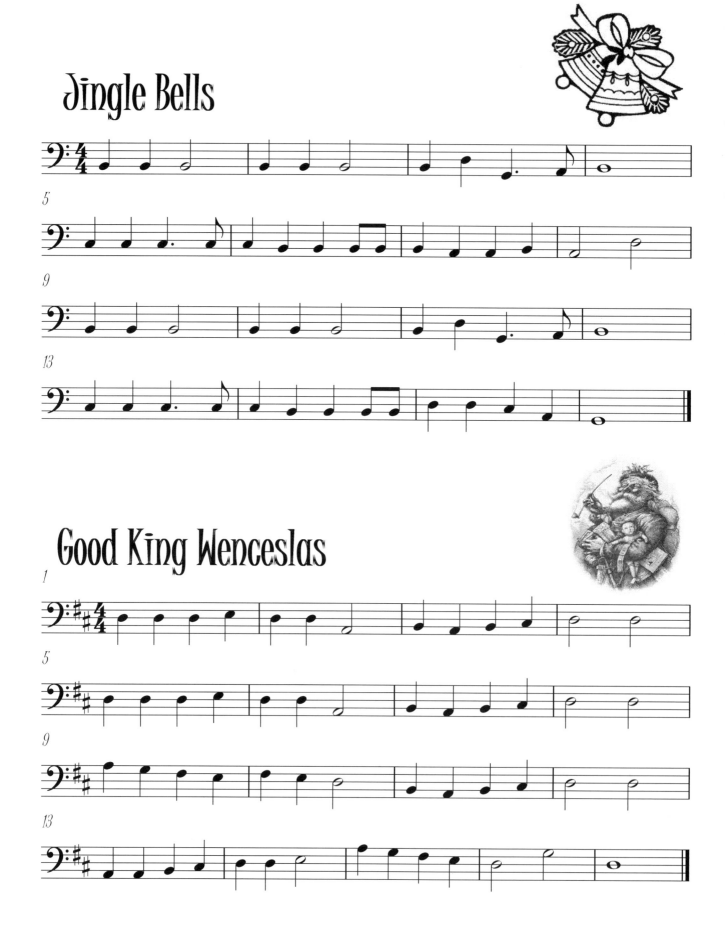

Good King Wenceslas

3

Silent Night

O Come All Ye Faithful

We Three Kings

God Rest Ye Merry Gentlemen

6

It Came Upon a Midnight Clear

Hark! The Herald Angels Sing

The First Nowell

Once in Royal David's City

The Holly and the Ivy

We Wish You a Merry Christmas

10

Deck the Halls

Twelve Days of Christmas

O Little Town of Bethlehem

Ding Dong Merrily on High

12

Joy to the World

Angels from the Realms of Glory

I Saw Three Ships

The Wexford Carol

Cherry Tree Carol

Wassail Song

Sans Day Carol

Sussex Carol

Down in Yon Forest

In Dulci Jubilo

18

Infant Holy, Infant Lowly

O Come, O Come, Emmanuel

Carol of the Drum

Gloucestershire Wassail

O'Carolan's Lament

Drive the Cold Winter Away

Il Est Ne, Le Divin Enfant

Part-a-Pan

In the Bleak Midwinter

Jingle Bells

Joyful and Jolly!

If you have enjoyed this book, why not try the other books in the series:
Introducing

Easy Traditional Duets   **Duets for**   **Easy Classics**   **Classic Duets**
(beginners +)   **Recorders**   **(teacher +**   **(Intermediate)**
                      (easy)   **beginner)**

Christmas Duets   **The Vibrant Violin**   **Easy Tunes**
and   **Book of Christmas**   **from Around**
More Christmas Duets   **Carols**   **the World**

50 Greatest Classics   **Trick or Treat**   **Catch the Beat**   **40+ Country**
                         A Halloween   **Sight Reading**   **Dance Tunes**
                         Suite   **(descant)**

Look out for more exciting music, playalongs and downloads at:

wildmusicpublications.com
@wmpublications

27660120R00018

Made in the USA
San Bernardino, CA
16 December 2015